The Relationship between Item Validity
and Test Validity

BY MAX SMITH

SUBMITTED IN PARTIAL FULFILLMENT OF THE REQUIREMENTS FOR
THE DEGREE OF DOCTOR OF PHILOSOPHY IN THE FACULTY
OF PHILOSOPHY, COLUMBIA UNIVERSITY

BUREAU OF PUBLICATIONS
Teachers College, Columbia University
NEW YORK CITY
1934

PRINTED IN
THE UNITED STATES OF AMERICA

THE RUMFORD PRESS
CONCORD, N. H.

G3060/31

Acknowledgments

I WISH to express my sincere appreciation to Dr. Irving Lorge for his never-failing help and advice during the entire course of the study, and to the members of my dissertation committee, Professors Ralph B. Spence, Henry A. Ruger, and Helen M. Walker, for their careful criticism of the manuscript.

I wish to express my gratitude, also, to Dr. Joseph Zubin for his aid in determining the spuriousness of the Pearson r between an item and a criterion when the item is part of the criterion; and to Professor Edward L. Thorndike and Dr. Ella Woodyard for their gracious permission to use the inventoried items of the Institute of Educational Research.

M. S.

Contents

CHAPTER   PAGE

   I. Do the Best Items Necessarily Form the Best Test?   1

  II. An Analysis of Some Published Data Relevant to the Problem 4

 III. Desirable Conditions for a Dependable Determination of the Usefulness of Item Validity Coefficients . 9

 IV. The Data and Their Preliminary Treatment . . . 13

  V. The Relative Validities of the "Best," the "High," the "Low," and the "Worst" Sub-tests 20

 VI. Suggestions Concerning the Method of Utilizing Item Validity Coefficients in Test Construction 25

VII. The Validity Obtained by Eliminating the Worst Items 27

VIII. Summary 32

Appendix. The Spuriousness of Bi-serial r When the Item Is Part of the Criterion 35

List of References 39

Tables

TABLE   PAGE

1. Distribution and Probable Error of Bi-serial Coefficients of Correlation for 200 Items 16

2. Range, Mean, and Standard Deviation of the Bi-serial Coefficients for Each Sub-test and for the Criterion 17

3. Distribution of Vocabulary Scores: 1930, 1931, and 1932 18

4. Mean and Standard Deviation of the Sub-test Scores and of the Criterion Scores: 1930, 1931, and 1932 19

5. Correlation of Each Sub-test with the Criterion: 1930, 1931, and 1932 21

6. Statistics for Determining the Significance of the Differences between Pairs of Correlations in Table 5 21

7. Intercorrelations among the 20-Item Sub-tests: 1930, 1931, and 1932 23

8. Correlation of the Criterion with Combinations of Sub-tests: 1930, 1931, and 1932 28

9. Statistics for Determining the Significance of the Differences between Pairs of Correlations in Table 8 . . . . ' . . . 29

10. Figures to Help Interpret the Increase in Validity Shown in Table 8 Obtained through Eliminating the "Worst" Sub-test 30

I

Do the Best Items Necessarily Form the Best Test?

THAT tests of capacity are of great value in the fields of guidance and of education may be assumed without discussion. The validity of such tests depends ultimately upon the items of which they are composed. The wise selection of test items is consequently a matter of great importance. The present study deals with one phase of item selection—the utilization of statistical item validity coefficients.

The historical background of methods used in item selection up to 1927 has been presented adequately by Barthelmess. ['31, pp. 3–10] * Until 1923, "statistical validation (of group tests) by correlation with a criterion was generally limited to test batteries and to sub-tests; the individual elements within a sub-test were chosen to give the maximum difficulty spread over the range desired, but were not individually validated by any correlation with the criterion." ['31, Barthelmess, p. 7]

In the development of the Otis Self-Administering Test (published October 1923) every item was individually validated by comparing the percents of accuracy of two widely varying groups of pupils. Apparently this was the first time that the individual elements of a group intelligence test were validated by comparison with a criterion other than chronological age.

Between 1924 and 1927 a number of investigators used or suggested various methods for validating individual test elements. Barthelmess' study is for the most part a statistical and logical analysis of most of these methods and some others she herself added. Her conclusions apparently proceed from the mathematical structure of the formulae used and from the data, and seem acceptable.

Furthermore, since 1927 other workers have investigated item validity coefficients. Cook ['32], in selecting spelling words,

---

* The List of References on page 39 is arranged according to year of publication, the arrangement within each year being alphabetical.

compared five indices of discrimination.   Lentz, Hirshstein, and Finch ['32] evaluated four still different item validity coefficients. On the basis of Barthelmess' study and these later investigations we may reasonably assume that for most situations a suitable technique is available for validating an individual test item against a given criterion.

However, even if the best item coefficient—whatever it may be—has been employed and the validity of the individual test items against a given criterion is known, then arises the problem: Do the most valid items form the most valid test?

At first thought one might be inclined to take for granted that the most valid items *do* form the most valid test; and that is just what most workers in the field seem to have done.   For example, the last reference cited, Lentz et al. ['32], begins as follows: "The importance of technique for selecting best items for inclusion in a test becomes greater and more apparent as measurement re-search increases.   A chain is reputedly only as strong as its weak-est link; while the weakest item in a test is not the sole determining factor of a test's strength, the analogy is suggestive, and we find it highly important to eliminate the weakest items."

The Commission on Scholastic Aptitude Tests of the College Entrance Examination Board apparently has been proceeding on the same assumption.   Using large numbers of cases, it has com-puted reliable bi-serial validity coefficients for many items, and has dropped the unsatisfactory ones. ['32, Brigham]

Likewise, Barthelmess, although she recognized the nature of the problem, accepted the assumption, writing: "Until further study shows how the practice can be improved, the method of building a test that will be assumed here will be based on the choice of elements showing the highest individual validities regardless of intercorrelations." ['31, pp. 36–38]

It is not necessarily true, however, that the most valid test is that formed by the items with the highest validity coefficients; for as soon as there is more than one item on a test, the total correlation of the test with a criterion becomes dependent on two kinds of factors: (a) the correlations between each item and the criterion, and (b) the intercorrelations among the items.   Just as is the case in ordinary multiple-correlation, the size of the total correlation varies in the same direction as the type (a) coefficients, but inversely to the type (b) correlations.

Thus it is theoretically possible that the best aggregate test is formed by items many of which rank low individually, if their mutual intercorrelations are relatively low enough. Or, perhaps, there is no appreciable difference between the goodness of the aggregate test formed from individually good items and that formed from individually poor ones. Then again, it may be that the good items do form the better total test.

The answer to the problem is of fundamental importance in test construction. If there is no significant difference, the laborious statistical evaluation of individual items might as well be dispensed with entirely (unless it is to be supplemented by elaborate intercorrelation studies). If the better items do form a sufficiently better test, item evaluation perhaps takes on an added importance.

Even in the latter case there is another aspect of the matter to be considered before the work of computing item validity coefficients is justified. Suppose that there is a significant relationship between the validity of the individual items and the validity of the test constructed from those items. Still it does not follow that the shorter test obtained by selecting the best items or by eliminating the poorest will be better than the complete original test which included all of them. If the original test is no worse, it might have been more economical to have kept on administering and scoring it without bothering about item validity coefficients at all.

According to the present study, only a very slight increase in validity may be expected from the use of item validity coefficients.

II

An Analysis of Some Published Data Relevant to the Problem *

So widespread has been the uncritical acceptance of the assumption that the items with highest validity will yield the best test, that practically no work has been done with the purpose of checking up on it. However, generally in connection with other problems, some data have been published which bear upon the question.

Abelson ['27], using as a criterion college grades with a reliability of .56, calculated for each of 40 items of the American Council Completion Test two McCall validity coefficients [1] based on two groups of 68 and 69 cases respectively. He then divided the 40 items into four sub-tests according to their validity coefficients computed from one group, and obtained the following correlations of each sub-test with the criterion, using the other group of cases:

Items	Correlation with the Criterion	
	Selection Based on First 68 Cases	Selection Based on Last 69 Cases
10 best items	.359	.031
Mediocre set (rank 16–25)	.391	.206
Mediocre set $\left\{ \begin{array}{l} \text{ranks } 11–15 \\ \text{and } 26–30 \end{array} \right\}$	.309	.272
10 worst items	.139	.050
All items	.340	.161

* In interpreting the various results quoted in this chapter, the reader may find it desirable first to familiarize himself with the concepts of the Fisher z-technique, discussed on pages 20 and 29.

$$[1] \quad C = \frac{(M_1 - M_2)\,(N_1 - N_2) + (M_1 - M_3)\,(N_1 - N_3) + (M_2 - M_3)\,(N_2 - N_3)\, \ldots, \text{etc.}}{S.D. \times N^2}$$

where:

C is the McCall validity coefficient;

M_1, M_2, M_3, etc., are in their order of size from highest to lowest, the means in terms of criterion score of the groups making respectively responses 1, 2, 3, etc., for the given item;

N_1, N_2, N_3, etc., are the frequencies of the respective responses;

$S.D.$ is the standard deviation of the entire group of which the response groups are component parts;

N^2 is the square of the frequency of the entire group ['27, Abelson, p. 83].

Item coefficients calculated from so small a number of cases are all but worthless; and the Pearson r's obtained for the sub-tests have high probable errors. Still, if any conclusion might be drawn, it would seem to be that the worst items form the worst test, but the best items do not form the best test.

Isaacs ['28], using as a criterion first year high school English marks, calculated for the 75 items of the Otis Self-Administering Test of Mental Ability, McCall validity coefficients based on 66 cases. Three sub-tests were formed from 45 of the items according to their validity coefficients, and the following correlations obtained using the same 66 cases:

15 best items	.284
15 mediocre items	.278
15 worst items	.086

The results, though lacking reliability, indicate so far as they go that although the worst items form the worst test, a test built from the mediocre items is not significantly inferior to one constructed from the best items.

Wolfe ['32] worked with 220 varied intelligence items of the Philadelphia Classification Test II furnished by Barthelmess. Using as a criterion a group of tests including the items under consideration, he calculated bi-serial r's for the 220 items based on 100 cases of elementary school children in the upper grades. Several sub-tests were constructed on the basis of item validities, and the following correlations with the criterion were obtained for a different 100 cases:

Nature of Test Items	Average Bi-serial r with Criterion $(N = 100)$	Total r with Criterion $(N = 100)$
Best 33	.839	.896
Next best 33	.704	.887
Worst 33	.103	.678

Again the worst items form somewhat the worst test, there being no significant difference between the test formed from the best items and that formed from the next best items although there is a marked difference in average item validity coefficient between them. Furthermore, the inferiority of the sub-test composed of the worst items is not nearly so pronounced as the average inferiority of the items which compose it. The true differences between sub-tests, however, are somewhat obscured by the fact that each sub-test forms part of the criterion against which it is evaluated; and the conclusions are weakened by the small number of cases on which they are based.

Concerning the second phase of the problem with which this study deals—the validity of the complete original test compared with that of the shorter test formed by eliminating a large or a small proportion of the items with the lowest validity coefficients —some of the data available seem more reliable. Schwesinger ['26] computed the Vincent percentage of overlap [2] for 1000 vocabulary 5-response items, the criterion being in each case a 200-item test containing the item, N averaging about 190 pupils in grades 5–9 of a small suburban town. Three hundred items with overlap of 6% or less were found and used in making forms A and B of the final test. The following correlations were computed:

No. of Tests	Nature of Each Test	Average Correlation with CAVD Criterion	Average Correlation with I.E.R. Word Knowledge Criterion	Cases on Which Each Correlation Is Based
5	200 unselected items	.859	.848	About 190 suburban pupils in grades 5–8
2	150 of the 300 "best" items	.882	.858	About 326 pupils in grades 5–8 of a metropolitan school

The improvement resulting from using only the 30% best items amounted to .02 in the Pearson r with one criterion and .01 with the other. Furthermore, only two forms of the test were left in place of the original five. Of course, the result—a test which is shorter but somewhat more valid—is desirable in itself, but it is questionable whether the actual gain justifies the effort involved in obtaining it.

Wheldon and Davies ['31], using average law grades for the year as the criterion, divided the items of eleven true-false tests into four groups on the basis of how well the items discriminated

[2] This is a method of comparing two groups which have a range of comparable scores, by finding the median of one group and computing the percentage of the second group which reaches or exceeds that median. In item validation, the two groups are (1) the total test scores of those who passed an item, and (2) the total test scores of those who failed it. The percentage of group (2) which reaches or exceeds the median score of group (1) is the Vincent "omd." The greater the amount of overlapping, the poorer the item ['24, Vincent, p. 9].

among the best third of the criterion group, the middle third, and the lowest third. The number of cases involved in deciding upon each item's classification is not given; neither is the number of items falling into each classification, nor the number of cases underlying the Pearson r's reported. No estimate can therefore be made of the reliability of the following results:

Examination	Correlation of Criterion with Entire True-False Test	Correlation of Criterion with the Discriminating Questions
1	.71	.81
2	.82	.87
3	.69	.78
4	.66	.69
5	.75	.84
6	.46	.58
7	.57	.72
8	.50	.75
9	.51	.81
10	.58	.67
11	.56	.71

In every case the shorter test obtained by eliminating the non-discriminating and reversely-discriminating items is more valid than the complete original test. Here item analysis seems to have been worth while, but unless we know the number of cases and the number of items, we can infer nothing more definite.

Poppel,[3] using Wolfe's data, compiled the following table, the bi-serial r's of the items being determined from 100 cases, and the correlations of the sub-tests calculated for a different group of 100:

Sub-test	Nature of Sub-test	Correlation with Criterion ($N = 100$)
1	33 items highest in validity	.895
2	66 " " " "	.932
3	86 " " " "	.922
4	106 " " " "	.924
5	126 " " " "	.938
6	146 " " " "	.947
7	166 " " " "	.949
8	186 " " " "	.951
9	206 " " " "	.948
10	220 " " " "	.947

[3] Table compiled by William Poppel in the course of his graduate work under Dr. Abelson at the College of the City of New York, 1931, and quoted in Wolfe's thesis ['32].

added together to give a composite measure. (e) Furthermore, the criterion scores should have a reliability coefficient approaching unity. Departure from perfect reliability in criterion scores tends to attenuate a validity coefficient computed against that criterion—consequently, to increase the probable error and reduce the significance of the obtained coefficient. Even if it is a complete test which is being validated and Pearson r is the coefficient used, it is, of course, desirable to minimize such loss of significance. In the case of item validation it is still more necessary that such loss in significance of the obtained item coefficients be kept down to a minimum, since item validity coefficients, even when based on hundreds of cases, have relatively high probable errors. (f) Any results obtained with the group from which the item coefficients were calculated should be checked with similar groups containing different individuals.

The present study is an attempt to discover, by a method which fulfills the conditions suggested, what relationship exists between the validity of a test and the validity of its items.

Condition (a): Bi-serial r^1 was the measure of item validity employed in the present study, although it is more laborious to obtain than most others. From a theoretical point of view, Symonds ['30] recommended bi-serial r as the most desirable item validity coefficient to use. Barthelmess ['31, p. 87], after an empirical and logical investigation of a number of item validity coefficients, concluded that when a dichotomous method is to be employed, the use of bi-serial r is the best method for validating individual test items. Cook ['32] concluded that bi-serial r was second in value among five indices of discrimination which he investigated empirically. The Commission on Scholastic Aptitude Tests has been using bi-serial r in its item analysis. So, too, has Thorndike, though he estimates its value from the percentage of overlap ['26, p. 122].

Condition (b): The item validity coefficients of this study are

---

[1] The formula of bi-serial r is $\dfrac{M_1 - M_2}{\sigma} \cdot \dfrac{pq}{z}$. In the present problem M_1 is the mean criterion score of those who "pass" the item; M_2, the mean criterion score of those who "fail" the item; σ, the standard deviation of the criterion scores of the entire group; and pq and z, constants obtained from a table of the normal curve depending on p, the proportion of the entire group which "passes" the item.

Assuming normality in the bi-variate distribution, bi-serial r corresponds to the ordinary Pearson r between two distributions. The formula was originally derived by Pearson in 1909. Its derivation is also given by Kelley ['23, pp. 245–49].

based on 370 cases. A larger group would have been preferable, but no other subjects were available to the author at the time the original data were collected.

Condition (c): Among the 200 bi-serial coefficients calculated, 2 were negative, the other 198 ranging from .02 to .91. The average bi-serial *r*'s of the four sub-tests formed from the "best," the "high," the "low," and the "worst" items were .76, .56, .44, and .16 respectively. Thus, as can be seen, there was a wide range of validity coefficients.

Condition (d): A vocabulary test was considered the best criterion to fulfill the fourth condition. Thorndike ['26, p. 183] has written: "Word knowledge is a specially suitable case for study, because it has been approved by Terman as one of the very best single measures of intellect, and is involved to some degree in many of our better tests, such as oral and printed directions, paragraph reading or comprehension, sentence completion, opposites, and other tests of relations presented in words." Studies by other investigators, such as Kelley ['28] and Brigham ['32, pp. 28–44], using tetrad analysis, have shown that "verbal ability" is a very important part of, and seems to be a specific factor in, the composite known as mental ability. And Schneck ['29, p. 48], investigating several different kinds of verbal tests, concluded, "The best single test of verbal ability is a vocabulary test." [2]

Consequently, we may consider the total vocabulary score as the measure of a specific capacity which each item more or less directly attempts to estimate.

Condition (e): Workers who have experimented with vocabulary tests have in general reported high reliability coefficients. In the present study the criterion against which the item coefficients were calculated had a self-correlation of about .97; that against which the sub-tests were evaluated, a reliability coefficient of about .94.

Condition (f): The results obtained from the original group were checked with two other groups of 542 and 527 cases respectively.

The six conditions postulated for obtaining a dependable indication of the relationship between item validity and test validity

[2] Several more recent investigations have found the antonyms test slightly superior even to the vocabulary test as a measure of verbal ability.

seem to have been met in a fairly satisfactory manner.   On the whole, then, it seems reasonable to assume that any consistent relationship between the validity of a sub-test and that of the items of which it is composed found in the present study will have sufficient reliability to serve as the basis for conclusions relevant to at least the sort of data involved.

IV

The Data and Their Preliminary Treatment

THE data for the investigation were obtained as follows: A 200-item vocabulary test was given to 400 subjects.[1] The score on the entire test was used as the criterion, and the bi-serial correlation of each item with the total score calculated.[2]

The items were then arranged according to the size of their bi-serial coefficients, and four aggregates of twenty formed as follows:

(a) The twenty items with the highest bi-serial r's (1–20). This aggregate will hereafter be called the "best" sub-test or sub-test 1.

(b) The twenty items with bi-serial r's ranking 61–80 inclusive. This aggregate will be referred to as the "high" sub-test or sub-test 2.

(c) The twenty items with bi-serial r's ranking 121–140 inclusive. This aggregate will be known as the "low" sub-test or sub-test 3.

(d) The twenty items with the lowest (including negative) bi-serial r's (181–200). These will be called the "worst" sub-test or sub-test 4.

The remaining 120 items (with bi-serial r's ranking 21–60, 81–120, and 141–180) constituted the "criterion" group.[3]

---

[1] Thirty test papers were later eliminated—5 because of faulty mimeographing and 25 because the last five or more items had not been attempted—leaving 370 for the study.

[2] In view of the fact that the score obtained on each item tends to contribute 1/200 of the total to the total score, the bi-serial r between each item and the criterion will have a spurious element. However, although the absolute values of the bi-serial coefficients are higher than those which would have been obtained had each item in turn been eliminated from the criterion score, the relative ranks for the 200 bi-serial r's will be exactly the same, except for a few theoretically *possible*, but unlikely and immaterial, interchanges between the rank of items which stand next to each other. Since the present study was concerned only with the relative order of the bi-serial correlations, the calculated coefficients were used without correction.

A method for estimating the numerical amount of the spuriosity is discussed in the Appendix.

[3] It is true that the 120-item criterion is not exactly the same as the 200-item criterion against which the bi-serial r's were calculated. However, in view of the fact that the correlation between the 120-item criterion and the whole 200-item test is .988, it is highly probable that if the

The problem now resolved itself into the question, How do these four tests compare with one another? Do the "best" twenty items form the best aggregate test? Do the "worst" twenty items form the worst aggregate test? How "good" is the test composed of the twenty "high" items? How good is that made up of the twenty "low" ones? The answer was found by obtaining the total correlation of each sub-test with the criterion, and by comparing with one another the correlation coefficients thus obtained.

The 200 items were selected from the many hundreds listed in the vocabulary item inventory of the Institute of Educational Research at Teachers College. This inventory gives for each item the percent of pupils in various grades succeeding with it, and an estimated difficulty level derived from all the statistics available. The items with CAVD difficulty levels from 367 to 390, of which there were about three hundred, seemed best suited to the group to be tested. Two hundred of these were chosen in such a way as to include fewer from the extremely easy and hard levels than from the intermediate levels. They were arranged in order of difficulty level, the easier coming first.

As it turned out, the difficulty range selected was well adjusted to the group to be tested. Theoretically the best difficulty level[4] for a test to be used with any group is such that the average score of that group is 50%. In a 5-response test where no correction is made for guessing, the optimum average would be halfway between 20% and 100%, or 60%. On the 200 vocabulary items, which were of the last type, the percents succeeding on each item varied from 21% to 93%, with a standard deviation of 15.4%, the average being 62.1%—as close to the optimum as could reasonably be expected. The arrangement also was fairly satisfactory, the correlation between the CAVD difficulty level of each of 200 items and the actual percentage of 370 students not succeeding on it being .472 ± .037.

On November 21, 1930, 278 boys in the last term of the elementary school (eighth year) and 122 in the last term of the

---

80 bi-serial *r*'s involved were recalculated using the 120-item criterion, not a single one would be shifted out of the "best," the "high," the "low," or the "worst" sub-tests to one of the other three sub-tests. (It must be kept in mind that any item in a sub-test is separated from the nearest item in any other sub-test by at least forty criterion items.) Consequently, the use of the 120-item criterion with the four sub-tests is quite valid for the purposes of this study.

[4] This matter is discussed by Symonds ['29].

junior high school (ninth year) took the vocabulary test as one of their entrance examinations to Townsend Harris High School, the preparatory school of the College of the City of New York. Elementary and junior high schools from all parts of New York City were represented.

Townsend Harris prepares its boys for college in either three or two and one-half years, and therefore attempts to select the brightest students possible. The principals in the elementary and junior high schools are requested to send only their best boys to take the qualifying examination; and take pains to do so. Consequently the 400 applicants were a highly selected group on the basis of school record. Their median proficiency grade was B+, which is significantly better than the average for the city. In age the pupils varied from 10 years 11 months to 17 years. The median age was 13 years 3 months; the lower quartile, 12 years 9 months; the upper quartile, 13 years 10 months.

The tests were administered by the author. Sufficient time was allowed for practically everyone to finish. The nature of the examination can be inferred from the directions and the first few items, which are here reproduced:

Look at the first word in line 1. Find the other word in the line which means the same or most nearly the same. Write its number at the end of the line. Do the same in lines 2, 3, 4, etc. Lines A, B, and C show the way to do it. Do all the lines. When you do not know, make a guess. Write some number for each line.

A. beast	1 afraid, 2 words, 3 large, 4 animal, 5 bird	..*4*..A.
B. baby	1 cradle, 2 mother, 3 little child, 4 youth, 5 girl	..*3*..B.
C. raise	1 lift up, 2 drag, 3 sun, 4 bread, 5 deluge	..*1*..C

1. conspire	1 plot, 2 breathe, 3 rely, 4 die, 5 outrun	..... 1.
2. antique	1 caper, 2 gaunt, 3 old, 4 queer, 5 indignant	..... 2.
3. hazardous	1 dangerous, 2 unbecoming, 3 accidental, 4 misty, 5 distinctive	..... 3.
4. compel	1 attack, 2 persuade, 3 oppose, 4 force, 5 offend	..... 4.
5. heedful	1 concise, 2 cheerful, 3 expressive, 4 careful, 5 repentant	..... 5.

The mean score of the 370 cases used in the item analysis is 124.78; the standard deviation (adjusted by Sheppard's correction), 33.49. The reliability coefficient of the test obtained by correlating odd-and even-numbered items and using the Spearman-Brown formula $\dfrac{(2r)}{(1+r)}$ is .9685; the probable error of measurement being 4.01 score points.

The bi-serial correlation with the total score was calculated for each of the 200 items. The distribution of these coefficients is shown in Table 1. They range from .9087 to −.1848, two of the coefficients being negative. The mean is .4895 and the corrected standard deviation, .1710. The probable errors of the coefficients vary from .0163 to .0555.

TABLE 1

Distribution and Probable Error of Bi-serial Coefficients of Correlation for 200 Items

Size of Coefficient	Range of Probable Errors * of the Actual Coefficients in the Interval	Frequency
.90–.99	.016	1
.80–.89	.025–.043	2
.70–.79	.024–.041	19
.60–.69	.028–.037	30
.50–.59	.032–.049	46 Mdn = .496
.40–.49	.035–.056	48 Mn = .490
.30–.39	.038–.054	27 Corrected σ = .1710
.20–.29	.042–.051	18
.10–.19	.043–.051	5
.00–.09	.048–.049	2
−.00– −.09	.043	1
−.10– −.19	.045	1
		N = 200

* The size of the probable error of bi-serial r depends upon the number of cases on which the r is based, the size of the r itself, and the proportion "passing" the item. The probable errors here given were calculated by the following formula, which gives a good approximation for values of p between .05 and .95: $P.E._r = \dfrac{.6745}{\sqrt{N}}\left(\dfrac{\sqrt{pq}}{z}-r^2\right)$. The range of p's in the present study was from .211 to .927.

The items were then subdivided into five groups on the basis of their bi-serial coefficients as explained on page 13. Table 2 gives for each of the five groups the range of bi-serial r's, and the mean and standard deviation of the coefficients in that group.

Finally every subject's score on each of the four sub-tests and on the 120-item criterion was obtained, the original score thus being broken up into five components.

TABLE 2

Range, Mean, and Standard Deviation of the Bi-serial Coefficients
for Each Sub-test and for the Criterion

Test	No. of Items	Range of r's	Mean r	σ of the r's
"Best" sub-test	20	.7117–.9087	.7550	.0490
"High" sub-test	20	.5368–.5769	.5560	.0126
"Low" sub-test	20	.4222–.4515	.4390	.0092
"Worst" sub-test	20	—.1848–.2732	.1610	.1197
Criterion	120	.2844–.7066*	.4943	.1231

* Exclusive of the range of the "low" and the "high" sub-tests.

The same 200 items were given on March 27, 1931 to 542 new applicants for admission to Townsend Harris, 377 from 8B, and 165 from 9B or RD, the rapid advance equivalent of 9B. In order to save clerical labor, the items were rearranged so that all the items in any sub-test were grouped together.[5] In this form of the test, items 1–20 were those of the "best" sub-test as determined by the 1930 bi-serial r's; 21–40, those of the "high" sub-test; 41–60, those of the "low" sub-test; 61–80, those of the "worst" sub-test; and 81–200, the items forming the criterion.

The 200 items were repeated once more on November 18, 1932 —this time in the identical order originally used in 1930. There were 527 applicants in 1932, 327 from 8B and 200 from 9B or RD.

As in 1930, the 1931 and 1932 tests were both administered by the author—under the same conditions and with the same directions as in the original year. The degree of similarity among the vocabulary scores of the three populations may be seen in Table 3.

[5] The matter of which items are included in a test is but one of the variables determining that test's validity for a given group of subjects. Other variables may be the blurring of certain items or parts of items on the test blank; the time allotment for the test; the conditions under which the test is administered—the printed or oral directions, the physical conditions, the possibility of cheating, etc.; the length of the test, involving fatigue or boredom factors; the order of the items on the test blank.

Since the purpose of the 1931 investigation was to compare the validity of certain selections of items in 1931 with their validity in 1930, all other variables except the choice of items should have been held as constant as possible. The rearrangement introduced a variation in order of items.

However, if there is no correlation between the order of an item and its bi-serial r, the rearrangement of the items should not influence the validity of the sub-tests containing them. For the 1930 test the actual correlation between the order of an item and its bi-serial r ($N = 200$) is —.088 ± .150—apparently low enough not to contra-indicate the 1931 rearrangement.

Nevertheless, it was later felt that it would have been preferable to have avoided introducing the factor of item rearrangement. It was partly for this reason, as well as because three consistent sets of results generally mean much more than two, that in 1932 the original test was repeated.

TABLE 3

Distribution of Vocabulary Scores: 1930, 1931, and 1932

Score	Frequency		
	1930	1931	1932
190–199	1	0	1
180–189	11	12	13
170–179	24	29	31
160–169	28	38	51
150–159	28	59	64
140–149	40	58	50
130–139	47	53	55
120–129	32	50	48
110–119	31	48	47
100–109	30	48	41
90–99	28	48	44
80–89	30	42	38
70–79	19	33	18
60–69	16	16	10
50–59	4	2	9
40–49	0	4	3
30–39	0	2	4
20–29	1	0	0
N	370	542	527
Proportion of 8B pupils	.695	.696	.620
Proportion of 9B or RD pupils	.305	.304	.380
Median	127.22	125.60	130.27
Mean	124.78	123.78	126.99
Corrected σ	33.49	32.11	33.04

The forms of distribution are alike in all three cases; and the differences between the means and standard deviations are not statistically significant, although it is likely that the 1932 group is slightly superior (probably because of the somewhat greater proportion of 9B or RD pupils).

Eventually, as with the 1930 group, each of the 1931 and 1932 papers was rescored to yield five components: the score on each of the four sub-tests (as determined by the 1930 bi-serial coefficients) and that on the 120-item criterion.

The means and the standard deviations of these five component scores for the three years are shown in Table 4. In every case the "best" sub-test is the easiest and shows the greatest spread of scores, the "high," "low," and "worst" sub-tests becoming progressively more difficult and narrower in range. The criterion test is about equivalent to the "low" sub-test with regard to average difficulty and the variance of scores.

TABLE 4

Mean and Standard Deviation of the Sub-test Scores and of the Criterion Scores: 1930, 1931, and 1932

Sub-test	No. of Items	1930 Data N =370		1931 Data N =542		1932 Data N =527	
		Mean	σ	Mean	σ	Mean	σ
"Best" sub-test	20	15.80	4.84	16.37	4.37	16.24	4.41
"High" sub-test	20	13.22	4.06	13.36	4.01	13.30	4.12
"Low" sub-test	20	12.20	3.61	12.21	3.59	12.25	3.56
"Worst" sub-test	20	11.56	2.31	11.29	2.27	11.85	2.38
Criterion divided by 6*	⅙ of 120	12.29	3.60	11.92	3.60	12.58	3.57

* The criterion statistics are divided by 6 so that they may be more easily compared with those obtained from the sub-tests.

One must not, however, leap to the conclusion that among these items the easier an item is, the better it is; for the correlation between easiness and bi-serial r (200 items, 1930) is only .2908. Part of this correlation is probably attributable to the fact that in a 5-response test the more difficult items tend to have a larger proportion of their correct responses due to guessing.

The progressive decrease in variance leads temporarily to the conclusion that the goodness of the tests may perhaps be dependent on the size of the average bi-serial r; since, of course, a test with a large variance has more chance to be discriminating than one with a smaller spread of scores. However, the discrimination may not be with regard to the capacity it is desired to test, so that the goodness of the sub-tests must be determined in some other way.

For each year, the score on the criterion items was used as the measure against which each of the four sub-tests was evaluated.

V

The Relative Validities of the "Best," the "High," the "Low," and the "Worst" Sub-tests

THE correlations with the criterion are given in Table 5 for 1930, 1931, and 1932, and for the three sets of data as a whole. In determining the significance of the differences among these correlation coefficients, the "z-technique"[1] recommended by R. A. Fisher ['32, pp. 175–184] was employed. The ratio $\dfrac{z_a - z_b}{\sigma z_a - z_b}$ is crucial to the interpretation. A difference of twice its own sigma would occur by chance only about once in twenty times and, as Fisher suggests, may be considered significant. If the ratio is less than 2, the difference may in general be ascribed to chance. Table 6 shows separately for each year and for the combined average of all years the ratio $\dfrac{z_a - z_b}{\sigma z_a - z_b}$ for the six possible pairings of the four r's involved.

Although all the results have, for convenience' sake, been presented together, the fundamental differences among them must not be overlooked. The choice of items for the sub-tests was based entirely on the 1930 data; and therefore the 1930 results may be in part due to chance factors which acted with a constant effect on particular items throughout the entire statistical treatment of that particular set of data. The 1931 and 1932 results, on the other hand, are free from such a possibility. Consequently, it is desirable to interpret the results for the several sets of data separately.

[1] $z = \frac{1}{2}\left\{\log_e (1+r) - \log_e (1-r)\right\}$. The distribution of r is not normal in small samples and even for large samples it remains far from normal for high correlations; the distribution of z tends toward normality. The distribution of r changes rapidly as its "true" value changes; consequently the difference between two r's divided by the sigma of that difference cannot be interpreted very definitely. The difference between two z's divided by the sigma of that difference, however, can readily be interpreted in terms of probability from a table of normal deviates; and the probabilities inferred apply directly to the differences between the original r's.

Regardless of the magnitude of r, $\sigma^2_z = N-3$, where N is the number of cases on which the r was based.

TABLE 5

Correlation of Each Sub-test with the Criterion: 1930, 1931, and 1932

Sub-test	Correlation of Sub-test with the Criterion			
	1930 Data $N = 370$	1931 Data $N = 542$	1932 Data $N = 527$	Weighted Average for All Three Years $N = 1433$ *
"Best" sub-test	.8471	.8194	.9202	.8717
"High" sub-test	.8691	.8636	.8972	.8782
"Low" sub-test	.8009	.8140	.8561	.8276
"Worst" sub-test	.4304	.4119	.4951	.4478

* The correlations were averaged by means of the "z-technique" recommended by Fisher ['32]. The number of "degrees of freedom" involved in computing each r is $N - 3$, so that the significance is reduced 3 cases for every correlation averaged in (except one).

From the 1930 results shown in Table 5 and interpreted by means of Table 6 we conclude that the worst individual items form the poorest aggregate test. However, the "best" items do not form the most valid aggregate—a group of intermediate items

TABLE 6

Statistics for Determining the Significance of the Differences between Pairs of Correlations in Table 5*

r's Compared ** $(r_a - r_b)$	1930 Data $N = 370$		1931 Data $N = 542$		1932 Data $N = 527$		Average of the Three Years $N = 1433$	
	$\sigma_{z_a - z_b} = .0738$ ‡		$\sigma_{z_a - z_b} = .0609$		$\sigma_{z_a - z_b} = .0618$		$\sigma_{z_a - z_b} = .0374$	
	$z_a - z_b$	$\dfrac{z_a - z_b}{\sigma_{z_a - z_b}}$	$z_a - z_b$	$\dfrac{z_a - z_b}{\sigma_{z_a - z_b}}$	$z_a - z_b$	$\dfrac{z_a - z_b}{\sigma_{z_a - z_b}}$	$z_a - z_b$	$\dfrac{z_a - z_b}{\sigma_{z_a - z_b}}$
$r_{15} - r_{25}$	− .0839	−1.14	− .1523	−2.50	.1393	2.25	− .0199	−0.53
$r_{15} - r_{35}$	.1446	1.96	.0162	0.27	.3183	5.15	.1598	4.27
$r_{15} - r_{45}$	.7853	10.64	.7170	11.77	1.0540	17.06	.8580	22.94
$r_{25} - r_{35}$	.2285	3.10	.1685	2.77	.1790	2.90	.1877	5.02
$r_{25} - r_{45}$	.8692	11.78	.8693	14.27	.9147	14.80	.8859	23.69
$r_{35} - r_{45}$	.6407	8.68	.7008	11.51	.7357	11.91	.6982	18.67

* If $\dfrac{z_a - z_b}{\sigma_{z_a - z_b}}$ is numerically greater than ± 2, the difference is considered significant.

** 1 = score on "best" sub-test.   4 = score on "worst" sub-test.
2 = score on "high" sub-test.   5 = criterion score.
3 = score on "low" sub-test.

‡ The value of $\sigma_{z_a - z_b}$ depends entirely on the number of cases on which z_a and z_b are based, regardless of the size of the z's involved. For each year's data, all the z's are based on the same number of cases. Consequently, $\sigma_{z_a - z_b}$ is the same for all the $z_a - z_b$'s in a column.

with fairly high bi-serial r's forming an aggregate which is slightly, but not significantly, superior according to the obtained figures. Even a group of intermediate items with relatively low bi-serial r's forms an aggregate whose inferiority to that formed by the individually best items is only on the border-line between significance and nonsignificance. Nevertheless, to repeat, the worst items do form by far the worst aggregate.

More specifically, the 1930 results may be stated in the following manner: The 20-item sub-test with bi-serial r's ranging from .71 to .91 was, if anything, slightly worse than the sub-test whose r's ranged from .54 to .58, and but little better than the aggregate whose r's ranged from .42 to .45. However, the sub-test with two r's negative ($-.18$ and $-.05$) and with the other eighteen ranging from .02 to .27 was definitely much the worst of the four.

The conclusions are corroborated by the 1930 figures in Table 7, the table which shows the intercorrelations among the 20-item sub-tests for the three years. Each 20-item sub-test may be considered as a secondary and minor criterion for comparing the other three sub-tests. Then the high intercorrelations among the "best," "high," and "low" sub-tests (.70–.78) and their consistently lower correlations with the "worst" sub-test (.40–.42) definitely reinforce the conclusions drawn from the total correlations with the criterion. Moreover, the size of the correlations involved—especially in relation to their probable errors— seems to indicate meaningfulness of the results.

However, if the same 200-item test be given to a similar but different group, will the "best," "high," "low," and "worst" sub-tests make the same relative showing when correlated with the 120-item criterion? If they do, the results already obtained take on added significance. If not, the conclusions are weakened, and may have to be materially revised.

The 1931 correlations are based on such a different but similar group of applicants. The 1931 coefficients in Table 5 rank in the same order as those of 1930; and Table 6 clearly corroborates the previous conclusion that the "worst" items form the worst aggregate. In the case of the other aggregates, however, the pertinent 1931 column of Table 6 apparently does not confirm the earlier conclusions as to the significance of the differences. The "high" sub-test now appears *significantly* best; while the "best" sub-test, though still second, is no longer significantly better than the "low" sub-test. And just as the 1930 rankings were corroborated by the intercorrelations among the sub-tests in Table 7, so, too, are the 1931 rankings confirmed by the 1931 intercorrelations (except that r_{34} is higher than r_{14} and r_{24}).

TABLE 7

Intercorrelations among the 20-Item Sub-tests: 1930, 1931, and 1932

		"Best" (1)	"High" (2)	"Low" (3)	"Worst" (4)
"Best" (1)	1930		.7815	.7001	.4064
	1931		.7822	.6912	.2966
	1932		.8945	.7256	.4452
"High" (2)	1930	.7815		.7421	.4209
	1931	.7822		.7449	.3684
	1932	.8945		.7316	.4393
"Low" (3)	1930	.7001	.7421		.4035
	1931	.6912	.7449		.4019
	1932	.7256	.7316		.4389
"Worst" (4)	1930	.4064	.4209	.4035	
	1931	.2966	.3684	.4019	
	1932	.4452	.4393	.4389	

Nevertheless, the lack of consistency in the results does not really signify all that at first sight it appears to. Although, as pointed out in the note on page 17, the relative validity of the various sub-tests was probably not materially altered by the re-arrangement of items, nevertheless their relative validities as measured by the 120-item criterion were affected. The 120 criterion items were made the last ones in Form E; the "best" sub-test comprised the first 20 items, which were therefore farthest from the criterion group; the "high" subtest, the next 20 items; the "low" sub-test, items 41–60; and the "worst" sub-test, the 20 items nearest the criterion. Thus it can be seen that because of the greater correlation existing in general between near-by groups of items than between groups more widely separated, the "best" sub-test is most penalized; the "high" sub-test less so; the "low" sub-test, favored; and the "worst" sub-test even more favored when validities are measured against the 120-item criterion.

Any reasonable correction of the 1931 validity coefficients for this tendency would only strengthen the conclusion that the worst items form by far the worst composite, since r_{45} becomes even lower.   Furthermore, r_{35} would be reduced by such a correction; r_{25}, raised; and r_{15}, raised markedly—thus bringing the results into conformity with those of 1930.

The 1932 data seem least open to criticism.   In the first place, any chance factors which might have operated in 1930 to bring about differences among bi-serial r's would not affect the 1932 sub-test scores.   Second, no rearrangement in the order of items was introduced into the set-up as in 1931.   Furthermore, as shown in Table 3, the 1932 group of applicants was similar to those of 1930 and 1931.

All the differences obtained from the 1932 column of Table 5 are shown in Table 6 to be statistically significant, and are corroborated by the 1932 intercorrelations in Table 7 (except that r_{23} is higher than r_{13}).   The conclusion that the "worst" items form much the worst sub-test is now verified beyond any reasonable doubt.   Moreover, the twenty items low in validity again form the sub-test which ranks third in goodness—unequivocally third this time, as in 1930.   However, in 1932 the "best" sub-test is the best, the "high" sub-test now having been shifted to second place with respect to validity.

In view of the fact that the results for the three years are not in exact conformity with one another, the correlations of each sub-test with the criterion were averaged [2] for the three years to form a basis for the final conclusions.   The average coefficients thus obtained are given in the last column of Table 5, and the significance of the various differences, in Table 6.

On the basis of these figures we may conclude that without doubt by far the worst sub-test is that in which there were two items with negative validity coefficients ($-.18$ and $-.05$), the other eighteen ranging from .02 to .27.   Much better, but definitely inferior to the remaining two sub-tests, is the "low" sub-test, with item validity coefficients ranging from .42 to .45.   Above $r = .53$, however, there is no demonstrated advantage in goodness due to a higher average bi-serial r, the sub-test with bi-serial r's ranging from .54 to .58 being about equal in validity to that whose r's ranged from .71 to .91.

[2] The averaging of the three correlation coefficients for each sub-test is justified by the fact that the 1930, 1931, and 1932 populations were essentially similar.   For the method of averaging correlations by the "z-technique," see Fisher ['32, pp. 175–84].

VI

Suggestions Concerning the Method of Utilizing Item Validity Coefficients in Test Construction

ALTHOUGH the foregoing conclusions seem valid for the particular population tested and the particular items used, their application to the general field of testing is far from obvious. As Brigham has shown ['32, pp. 356–59], although bi-serial r's are stable for similar populations if based on a large number of cases, they are not comparable for different sorts of populations. Consequently, even if the obtained relationship between item validity and sub-test validity holds for other types of population and for different kinds of items, it does not follow that any particular sub-test found best for one group will be superior for other populations. At most, then, any application of the results can be expected to yield, not a generally superior test, but only one which is more valid for a particular type of population and against a particular criterion.

Moreover, before suggestions leading to even such improvement may be made with some degree of confidence, we should have to know whether in totally different situations relationships exist between item validity and test validity similar to those found in this study. Some data on this point which, though not very reliable, are suggestive have been presented in Chapter II.

In view of the evidence, poor as it is on the whole, it seems reasonable to conclude tentatively that the relationship found in this study between item validity and test validity will probably hold true, more or less, with other data. What application, then, can be made to the field of test construction?

In the case where a test maker has available a large number of items with item validity coefficients already calculated, there are two main methods of utilizing these coefficients: (1) to form alternate forms from the thirty or so percent of "best" items only, discarding all the others—as was done by Schwesinger ['26]; (2) to eliminate the twenty-five or so percent of "worst" items, forming the alternate forms from the remaining ones.   The latter procedure will yield a larger number of equivalent forms of the test about as valid in general as those formed by the best items only. Consequently the second procedure is indicated, since the first wastes unnecessarily a large proportion of the available items.

One cannot be definite about the proportion of worst items to drop, because that depends largely upon the sagacity and care employed in the original choice or construction of items, which will determine the proportions of items of varying validity.   And one cannot be specific about the size of validity coefficients below which items may well be eliminated, since that depends on the nature of the coefficient used, the reliability of the criterion, and the variability of the group.

When bi-serial r is the coefficient employed, Thorndike has written ['26, p. 129]: "It is a sound rule not to use any single task in a composite unless its r_{ti}, or the average r_{ti} for tasks like it, is above .30 for a school-grade population of the level for which it is intended.

"More precisely, for any two minutes of work we should obtain r_{ti} above .40 for grades 3 to 5; .35 for grades 6 to 8; .30 for grades 9 to 11; and .20 for grades 12 to 14.   It is harder to get high correlations in the higher grades, where the range of intellect may be narrower and where the specialization of the environment is greater."

The results of the present study would lead us to believe that these standards are too lenient for vocabulary items, a bi-serial r of approximately .40 being indicated for acceptable tasks at the grade 9 to 11 level if the criterion has a reliability of about .95.

VII

The Validity Obtained by Eliminating the Worst Items

IN the last chapter, a suggestion was evolved respecting the selection of items for alternate forms of a test when a large number of items with reliable validity coefficients is available. However, the question of whether it would have been worth the trouble in the first place to calculate such coefficients has not yet been answered.

Although the conclusion that the worst items formed by far the worst sub-test has been definitely proved, it does not yet follow that the labor of item analysis was justified. The existence of some definite relationship between the validity of a sub-test and that of the items of which it is composed is a necessary condition to justify item analysis work, but is not a sufficient one.

That the absence of such a relationship would render item validity coefficients useless can readily be seen. We are interested ultimately only in the validity of the total test used, and if there is no practical relationship between that validity and the validity coefficient of the items, it is of no use to know the latter.

That the existence of the marked relationship already found does not form a sufficient justification for statistical item analysis is not so obvious. But the crucial problem really is: What *improvement* in total validity can be obtained by the use of item validity coefficients? Even though the worst items form by far the worst aggregate, will the elimination of these items from the total test yield a greater total validity? If so, will the subsequent elimination of the "low" items, which formed a sub-test significantly inferior to the "high" and "best" sub-tests, increase the validity still more?

Table 8 gives for each of the three years and for the average of all three the correlation with the criterion of the entire 80 items, of the 60-item test formed by eliminating the "worst" items, and of the 40-item test left after eliminating also the "low" items.

Table 9 gives the statistics necessary to interpret the differences between these correlations.[1]

The results are similar for all three sets of data. In every case the 60-item test formed by eliminating the 20 worst items is slightly, but not significantly, more valid than the complete test of 80 items. Furthermore, in every case, when the 20 "low" items are then eliminated from the 60-item test, the 40-item test remaining is definitely less valid than the 60-item test including the low items; it is also less valid than the complete test of 80 items.

TABLE 8

Correlation of the Criterion with Combinations of Sub-tests: 1930, 1931, and 1932

Combination of Sub-tests*	r of Criterion with the Combination of Sub-tests							
	1930 Data N =370		1931 Data N =542		1932 Data N =527		Average of the three Years ** N =1433	
	r	Δ‡	r	Δ	r	Δ	r	Δ
1+2+3+4	.9131		.9119		.9564		.9321	
		+.0097		+.0032		+.0065		+.0066
1+2+3	.9228		.9151		.9629		.9387	
		−.0155		−.0248		−.0289		−.0260
1+2	.9073		.8903		.9340		.9127	

* 1 =score on "best" sub-test.   3 =score on "low" sub-test.
2 =score on "high" sub-test.   4 =score on "worst" sub-test.
** The correlations were averaged by means of the "z-technique" recommended by Fisher ['32]. The number of "degrees of freedom" involved in computing each r is N—3, so that the significance is reduced 3 cases for every correlation averaged in (except one).
‡ Δ is the difference between an r and the r immediately above it.

Both of these differences are significant when the data are considered as a whole. It follows, therefore, that the item validity coefficients (if already calculated) should have been used to eliminate the "worst" items, but not the "low" items.

But were the item coefficients worth calculating? To say that the improvement in validity when the 20 worst items are omitted averages .0066 points of correlation does not tell the whole story; for the meaning of a given improvement in a correlation coefficient depends upon the size of the coefficient. Thus an improvement

[1] See page 20 for a brief explanation of the nature of these statistics. For a fuller explanation see Fisher ['32, pp. 175–84].

from .90 to .99 would mean very much more than an increase from .30 to .39. In order to interpret consistently any gain or loss in a correlation coefficient, the difference should be expressed in terms of z-values. A given difference between two z-values signifies an approximately constant probability of obtaining such a difference by chance, regardless of the size of the coefficients involved.[2]

The gain in the size of the correlation coefficient obtained by eliminating the 20 worst items amounts to .0097 for 1930, .0032 for 1931, and .0065 for 1932. The differences in z-value to which

TABLE 9

Statistics for Determining the Significance of the Differences between Pairs of Correlations in Table 8*

r's Compared** $(r_a - r_b)$	1930 Data $N = 370$		1931 Data $N = 542$		1932 Data $N = 527$		Average of the three years $N = 1433$	
	$\sigma_{z_a - z_b} = .0738‡$		$\sigma_{z_a - z_b} = .0609$		$\sigma_{z_a - z_b} = .0618$		$\sigma_{z_a - z_b} = .0374$	
	$z_a - z_b$	$\dfrac{z_a - z_b}{\sigma_{z_a - z_b}}$	$z_a - z_b$	$\dfrac{z_a - z_b}{\sigma_{z_a - z_b}}$	$z_a - z_b$	$\dfrac{z_a - z_b}{\sigma_{z_a - z_b}}$	$z_a - z_b$	$\dfrac{z_a - z_b}{\sigma_{z_a - z_b}}$
$r_{5(1+2+3)} - r_{5(1+2+3+4)}$	.0614	0.832	.0193	0.317	.0824	1.333	.0532	1.422
$r_{5(1+2)} - r_{1(1+2+3)}$	−.0951	−1.289	−.1348	−2.213	−.2951	−4.775	−.1833	−4.901
$r_{5(1+2)} - r_{5(1+2+3+2)}$	−.0337	−0.457	−.1155	−1.897	−.2127	−3.442	−.1301	−3.479

* If $\dfrac{z_a - z_b}{\sigma_{z_a - z_b}}$ is numerically greater than ±2, the difference is printed in black type and may be considered significant.

** 1 = score on "best" sub-test.   4 = score on "worst" sub-test.
   2 = score on "high" sub-test.   5 = criterion score.
   3 = score of "low" sub-test.

‡ The value of $\sigma_{z_a - z_b}$ depends entirely on the number of cases on which z_a and z_b are based, regardless of the size of the z's involved. For each year's data, all z's are based on the same number of cases. Consequently, $\sigma_{z_a - z_b}$ is the same for all the $z_a - z_b$'s in a column.

these figures correspond are .0614, .0193, and .0824 respectively. In order that the meaning of these z-differences may the more readily be grasped, Table 10 has been prepared. Thus Table 10 shows that the 1930 z-difference of .0614, which represents a gain of .0097 points of correlation in Table 8 because $r_{5(1+2+3+4)}$ actually is .9131, would represent a gain of .0378 points of correlation if $r_{5(1+2+3+4)}$ were .6000, or a gain of .0300 points if

[2] Since z-values are distributed in a virtually normal manner, the differences between z-values are also so distributed. For a discussion of the type of distribution of z, see Fisher ['32, pp. 175–84]. An explanation of why the differences between two normally distributed variables are themselves normally distributed will be found in Yule ['29, pp. 318–22].

$r_{5(1+2+3+4)}$ were .7000, etc. Similarly, we see from the 1932 column in Table 10 that although eliminating the 20 worst items increased the actual correlation in Table 8 only .0065 points, had the original correlation of the criterion with the complete 80-item test been only .6000 instead of .9564, the increase in the size of the correlation coefficient would have been .0501—apparently eight times as large as that actually obtained.

Does the improved validity of the shortened test, obtained by eliminating the "worst" items, shown in Table 8 and interpreted by means of Tables 9 and 10, justify the labor of item analysis?

TABLE 10

Figures to Help Interpret the Increase in Validity Shown in Table 8 Obtained through Eliminating the "Worst" Sub-test

Assumed Size of $r_{5(1+2+3+4)}$	Amount of Increase in $r_{5(1+2+3)}$* under the condition assumed			
	1930 Data	1931 Data	1932 Data	Average of the Three Years
	$z_a - z_b = .0614$**	$z_a - z_b = .0193$	$z_a - z_b = .0824$	$z_a - z_b = .0532$
.6000	.0378	.0122	.0501	.0329
.7000	.0300	.0097	.0397	.0261
.8000	.0210	.0069	.0278	.0184
.9000	.0110	.0036	.0145	.0096
.9500	.0056	.0019	.0073	.0050

* $r_{5(1+2+3)}$ is the correlation of the criterion with the 60-item test obtained by eliminating the 20 items of the "worst" sub-test from the complete original test of 80 items.
** z_a is $z_{5(1+2+3)}$; z_b is $z_{5(1+2+3+4)}$.

It is very hard to say.   The answer will depend in any particular case on the care with which the items have been constructed or selected, on the extent to which the test will be used, and on the nature of the facilities available to the investigator for shortening the calculation of item coefficients.

If the selection or construction of the original test is such that it may include a number of items of unsuspected negative validity, the elimination of such items would almost certainly yield a more sizable improvement in validity than that obtained in this research.   Consequently, statistical item analysis may be justified if very many hastily constructed items are to be tried out, or perhaps if material of a totally new sort is included.   However, in general, a moderate amount of insight combined with care in the original selection of items will eliminate most items of negative validity.

If the test will be widely used, the total time saved in the administration and scoring of a shorter test might justify the expenditure of a good deal of time in preliminary item work even if there were no gain in validity, provided that there was no loss in validity. And, of course, any incidental gain in validity, even one so slight as that obtained in this study, is all to the good. However, if a test is to be used relatively infrequently, the time expended in item analysis can not, in general, be expected to yield proportionately valuable results.

Still, even in the latter case, if the investigator had access to a Hollerith printing counter with its approximately 720 "man power" in calculating Pearson r's for items, the calculation of item validity coefficients might be justified in order to shorten the test in accordance with the findings of the present study.

So far as obtaining more and more valid instruments of measurement is concerned, however, statistical evaluation of individual items apparently has little to contribute.

Perhaps if item validity coefficients are supplemented by intercorrelations among items, the desired gain in validity may be attained. Toops and Royer ['32] have been experimenting in this connection upon items already carefully selected, using a Hollerith printing counter to expedite the enormous amount of calculation involved. Their results have not yet been published.[3]

But the use of item validity coefficients alone increases validity very little (at any rate with items already well chosen). Certainly it does not furnish the automatic guarantee of validity improvement which has generally been assumed.

[3] Since this was written Horst ['34] has published results showing phenomenal improvement in validity through the use of a statistical method which takes account of the intercorrelations among items. The mathematical and statistical theory underlying the method are developed in the second of the two articles cited, the first being a non-mathematical presentation.

VIII

Summary

THERE were two phases to the problem under investigation: (a) What relationship exists between the validity of a sub-test and the validity of the individual items of which it is composed? (b) If some significant relationship is found, can it be used to raise significantly the validity of the original complete test?

A 200-item vocabulary test with a self-correlation coefficient of .97 was administered in 1930 to 370 bright eighth and ninth year pupils. For each of the 200 items a validity coefficient (bi-serial r) with the total score was calculated, two low negative coefficients and a wide range of positive ones resulting. The items were then ranked according to these coefficients. Four 20-item sub-tests and a 120-item criterion were formed on the basis of the ranks: the "best" sub-test from the 20 items ranking 1–20 in validity, the "high" sub-test from the items ranking 61–80, the "low" sub-test from those ranking 121–140, and the "worst" sub-test from those ranking 181–200. The remaining 120 items constituted the criterion for measuring the validity of the four sub-tests.

In 1931 the 200 items were again administered, in rearranged order, to an equivalent group of 542 pupils. In 1932 they were once more repeated, this time in the original order, with a similar population of 527 pupils. In both cases the "best," the "high," the "low," and the "worst" sub-tests as well as the criterion were composed of the same items which constituted the corresponding sub-test in 1930—as determined by the 1930 validity coefficients.

For each of the three years the "best" sub-test was the easiest and showed the greatest spread of scores, the "high," the "low," and the "worst" sub-tests becoming progressively more difficult and narrower in range. Although a sub-test with a large variance has more chance to be discriminating than one with a smaller spread of scores, the apparent conclusion that the goodness of a sub-test varies directly with its average validity coefficient does not follow, since the discrimination may not be with regard to the capacity it is desired to test.

The score on the criterion items was used as the measure against which each of the four sub-tests was evaluated, the "z-technique" recommended by R. A. Fisher being used to interpret the differences between correlations with the criterion. On the basis of the 1439 cases of the combined data, the conclusion was reached that by far the least valid sub-test was that with two bi-serial r's negative ($-.18$ and $-.05$) and with the other eighteen ranging from .02 to .27. Much better, but definitely inferior to the remaining two, was the "low" sub-test, with bi-serial r's ranging from .42 to .45. Above $r = .53$, however, there was no demonstrated advantage in goodness due to a higher average bi-serial r, the sub-test with bi-serial r's ranging from .54 to .58 being about equal in validity to that whose r's ranged from .71 to .91.

The foregoing conclusions were, in general, corroborated by the intercorrelations among the sub-tests for each of the three years.

On the basis of the relationship found between the validity of a sub-test and the validity of the individual items comprising it, the author made the following suggestion: In using item validity coefficients to construct alternate forms of a test, the test maker will find it more economical and no less effective to concentrate on eliminating the "worst" items rather than on utilizing only the "best" ones.

The author could give no general suggestion as to the specific proportion of items to be dropped, or the exact size of validity coefficients below which items might well be eliminated, since too many factors would be involved in any individual situation. He did conclude, however, that a bi-serial r of approximately .40 might be considered a minimum for acceptable vocabulary 5-response items at the grade 9 to 11 level if the criterion has a reliability of about .95.

With regard to the second phase of the problem under investigation—improving the validity of the original test by discarding items—the same 120-item criterion was of course used, the 80 items of the four sub-tests being considered the complete test to be studied. For each of the three sets of data, the 60-item test formed by eliminating the 20 worst items was slightly, but not significantly, more valid than the complete test of 80 items. However, when the 20 "low" items were also eliminated, the

40-item test remaining was significantly less valid than either the 60-item test including the "low" items or the complete test of 80 items.   Consequently, item validity coefficients (if already calculated) should have been used to eliminate the "worst" items, but not the "low" items.

In view of the relatively slight validity improvement obtained by their use, it seems that in many instances it would hardly be worth while to compute item validity coefficients.   Under special conditions, however—if there were many items of negative validity, if the test were to be very widely used, or if the investigator had extraordinary facilities for computing item coefficients— such computation might be justified.   But the use of item validity coefficients alone does not constitute a philosopher's stone capable of automatically transmuting our instruments of measurement into more and more valid ones.

APPENDIX

The Spuriousness of Bi-serial r When the Item Is Part of the Criterion

IF a test population is of approximately normal distribution, the bi-serial correlation with a valid criterion of the ability to be tested is generally accepted as the best standard for judging any single item's statistical validity when that item is scored dichotomously. Most test populations do tend toward the normal. The main difficulty generally is to obtain a reliable, valid criterion of the ability which the item is designed to measure.

A test item is generally administered as one of a battery of similar items. If these items are sufficiently numerous and well chosen on the whole, the aggregate score on all of them frequently furnishes a far better criterion of the underlying ability which it is desired to measure than any other available. "Well chosen" implies that the test as a whole correlates highly with other criteria of the ability; such as, in the case of verbal intelligence, for example, teachers' judgments, school marks, age-grade progress, other intelligence tests, etc.

The use of such an aggregate score as a criterion, however, tends to make the resultant coefficient larger than would be the case if an outside criterion were employed—toward the score of which success on the individual item under consideration would not contribute.

In the case of the present investigation this factor of spuriousness does not matter, because the relative rank of the coefficients (with possible, but negligible exceptions) is not affected. But if it is wished to compare bi-serial coefficients obtained from outside criteria with those obtained by using the total test score as the criterion, some estimate of the numerical amount of the spuriosity is desirable.

The obtained bi-serial r with the total score including the item $= \dfrac{m_2 - m_1}{\sigma_y} \cdot \dfrac{pq}{z}$. The criterion score of each "pass" will obviously be 1 point less if the item is not counted, while the criterion score of each "fail" will not be affected at all. Consequently the desired bi-serial coefficient of the response to each item with the score on all the *other* items of the test—excluding itself—will be:

$$r' = \frac{(m_2 - 1) - m_1}{\sigma_{(y-x)}} \cdot \frac{pq}{z} = \frac{\sigma_y}{\sigma_{(y-x)}}\left(r - \frac{pq}{z} \cdot \frac{1}{\sigma_y}\right),$$

where x stands for the score on the item, and r for the spurious, obtained coefficient.

If we assume that $\sigma_{(y-x)}$ is about equal to σ_y, the amount of spuriosity would approximate $\frac{1}{\sigma_y} \cdot \frac{pq}{z}$. With a large σ_y, this is numerically small, since the value of $\frac{pq}{z}$ is at most .6666—when $p = .50$ (at $p = .999$, $\frac{pq}{z} = .2967$). Thus, for the data of the present investigation ($\sigma_y = 33.49$), the maximum amount of spuriosity in any bi-serial r is about .02.

As a matter of fact, $\sigma_{(y-x)}$ will be progressively smaller than σ_y as the obtained bi-serial r grows larger; consequently, so will the difference of the obtained bi-serial r from the true r' with the score on all the *other* items. Furthermore, $\frac{pq}{z}$ will usually be smaller than its maximum value. Thus the actual numerical value of the spuriosity in the reported bi-serial coefficients will tend to be less than .02 for these data.

The following more rigorous exposition yields the same specific conclusions as to the amount of spuriosity in the obtained coefficients of this study, incidentally furnishing an expression for bi-serial r in terms of Pearson r.

The derivation will first be made in terms of the product-moment r, and later transformed into the corresponding bi-serial r expression.

Let $x =$ the item score, and $y =$ the total test score, including the item. $r =$ the obtained product-moment correlation between the item-response and the total test score; $r' =$ the desired correlation between the item-response and the test score excluding the item itself.

Then

$$r' = r_{x(y-x)} = \frac{\Sigma x(y-x)}{N_{\sigma_x \sigma_{(y-x)}}} = \frac{\Sigma xy - \Sigma x^2}{N_{\sigma_x \sigma_{(y-x)}}} = \frac{N r \sigma_x \sigma_y - N \sigma_x^2}{N \sigma_x \sigma_{(y-x)}} = \frac{r \sigma_y - \sigma_x}{\sigma_{(y-x)}}$$

$$= \frac{r \sigma_y - \sqrt{pq}}{\sqrt{\sigma_y^2 - 2r\sigma_y\sqrt{pq} + pq}} = \frac{r - \dfrac{\sqrt{pq}}{\sigma_y}}{\sqrt{1 - 2r\dfrac{\sqrt{pq}}{\sigma_y} + \left(\dfrac{\sqrt{pq}}{\sigma_y}\right)^2}}$$

When $p \neq 0$ or 1, and $\sigma_y \neq 0$, as is the case in any practical situation, the amount of spuriosity in the obtained r depends upon (a) the ratio of r to $\dfrac{\sqrt{pq}}{\sigma y}$, and (b) the ratio of $\sqrt{pq}$ to σy.

In the case of bi-serial r, the constants entering into these determining ratios are somewhat different. To avoid confusion, the obtained bi-serial r will be designated by Bi, and the "true" bi-serial r by Bi'. The subscript p refers to those "passing" the item: q to those "failing." $\overline{Y}$ is the mean of the Y's.

Then
$$Bi_{xy} = \frac{\overline{Y}p - \overline{Y}q}{\sigma_y} \cdot \frac{pq}{z} = \frac{\overline{Y}p - \dfrac{N\overline{Y} - \Sigma Yp}{qN}}{\sigma_y} \cdot \frac{pq}{z}$$

$$= \frac{1/q(\overline{Y}_p - \overline{Y})}{\sigma_y} \cdot \frac{pq}{z} = \frac{p(\overline{Y}_p - \overline{Y})}{\sigma_y} \cdot \frac{1}{z}$$

But
$$r_{xy} = \frac{\Sigma X Y - \dfrac{\Sigma X \Sigma Y}{N}}{N \sigma_x \sigma_y} = \frac{\Sigma Y_p - \dfrac{pN(N\overline{Y})}{N}}{N \sigma_x \sigma_y}$$

$$= \frac{pN\overline{Y}p - pN\overline{Y}}{N\sqrt{pq}\,\sigma_y} = \frac{p(\overline{Y}p - \overline{Y})}{\sigma_y} \cdot \frac{1}{\sqrt{pq}}$$

$\therefore \qquad Bi = r\dfrac{\sqrt{pq}}{z}$

Similarly $Bi' = r'\dfrac{\sqrt{pq}}{z}$, and $Bi' - Bi = \dfrac{\sqrt{pq}}{z}(r' - r)$.

Consequently the amount of spuriosity in the obtained Bi depends upon (a) the ratio of Bi to $\dfrac{pq}{z} \cdot \dfrac{1}{\sigma y}$, and (b) the ratio of $\dfrac{pq}{z}$ to σy.

If $Bi = +\frac{pq}{z\sigma}$ $\left(\text{i.e. if } r = \frac{\sqrt{pq}}{\sigma}\right)$, then $Bi' = 0$, and the amount of spuriosity in the obtained $Bi = \frac{pq}{z\sigma}$. If $Bi = +\frac{1}{2}\frac{pq}{z\sigma}$, then $Bi' = -\frac{1}{2}\frac{pq}{z\sigma}$, and again the spuriosity in the obtained $Bi = \frac{pq}{z\sigma}$. As Bi becomes greater than $\frac{pq}{z\sigma}$, the amount of spuriosity in Bi becomes smaller. As Bi becomes smaller than $\frac{1}{2}\frac{pq}{z\sigma}$ (in the algebraic sense, where $-.5$ is smaller than $+.1$), then too, the amount of spuriosity in Bi becomes smaller. For values of Bi between $\frac{1}{2}\frac{pq}{z\sigma}$ and $\frac{pq}{z\sigma}$, Bi' is negative, and the amount of spuriosity in Bi will be slightly larger than $\frac{pq}{z\sigma}$.

Thus we arrive again at the conclusion that for the data of the present investigation, the maximum amount of spuriosity in any bi-serial r is about .02.

However, if the σ of a total score be relatively small, say 10 points or less, the amount of spuriosity in any obtained bi-serial r may be fairly large.

If the actual value of Bi', the bi-serial correlation between the item and the test score excluding the item itself, is desired, it can be obtained as follows:

$$\frac{z}{\sqrt{pq}}\,Bi = \frac{\dfrac{z}{\sqrt{pq}}Bi - \dfrac{\sqrt{pq}}{\sigma_y}}{\sqrt{1 - 2Bi\dfrac{z}{\sqrt{pq}}\dfrac{\sqrt{pq}}{\sigma_y} + \left(\dfrac{\sqrt{pq}}{\sigma_y}\right)^2}}$$

$$Bi' = \frac{Bi - \dfrac{pq}{z\sigma_y}}{\sqrt{1 - 2Bi\dfrac{z}{\sigma_y} + \left(\dfrac{\sqrt{pq}}{\sigma_y}\right)^2}}$$

List of References

'23 KELLEY, TRUMAN L. *Statistical Method.* Macmillan Company.

'24 VINCENT, LEONA. *A Study of Intelligence Test Elements.* Contributions to Education, No. 152. Bureau of Publications, Teachers College, Columbia University.

'26 SCHWESINGER, G. C. *The Social-Ethical Significance of Vocabulary.* Contributions to Education, No. 211. Bureau of Publications, Teachers College, Columbia University.

'26 THORNDIKE, EDWARD L. *The Measurement of Intelligence.* Bureau of Publications, Teachers College, Columbia University.

'27 ABELSON, HAROLD H. *The Improvement of Intelligence Testing.* Contributions to Education, No. 273. Bureau of Publications, Teachers College, Columbia University.

'27 SNEDDEN, DONALD S. *A Study in Disguised Intelligence Tests.* Contributions to Education, No. 291. Bureau of Publications, Teachers College, Columbia University.

'28 CLARK, E. J. "A Method of Evaluating the Units of a Test." *Journal of Educational Psychology,* 19: 263–65.

'28 ISAACS, ARCHIE E. "An Evaluation of the Otis Self-Administering Test of Mental Ability in Terms of High School English Marks." Unpublished Master's Thesis, No. 46. School of Education, College of the City of New York.

'28 KELLEY, TRUMAN L. *Crossroads in the Mind of Man.* Stanford University Press, Stanford University, California.

'29 SCHNECK, MATTHEW M. *Measurement of Verbal and Numerical Abilities.* Archives of Psychology, No. 107. Columbia University.

'29 SYMONDS, PERCIVAL M. "Choice of Items for a Test on the Basis of Difficulty." *Journal of Educational Psychology,* 20: 481–93.

'29 YULE, G. U. *An Introduction to the Theory of Statistics,* Ninth Edition. Charles Griffin and Company, London.

'30 SYMONDS, PERCIVAL M. "A Comparison of Statistical Measures of Overlapping with Charts for Estimating the Value of Bi-serial r." *Journal of Educational Psychology,* 21: 586–96.

'31 BARTHELMESS, HARRIET M. *The Validity of Intelligence Test Elements.* Contributions to Education, No. 505. Bureau of Publications, Teachers College, Columbia University.

'31 LARSON, SELMER C. "The Shrinkage of the Coefficient of Multiple Correlation." *Journal of Educational Psychology,* 22: 45–55.

'31 WHELDON, CHESTER H. AND DAVIES, F. J. J. "A Method for Judging the Discrimination of Individual Questions on True-False Examinations." *Journal of Educational Psychology*, 22: 290–306.

'32 BRIGHAM, CARL C. *A Study of Error.* College Entrance Examination Board, 431 West 117th Street, New York City.

'32 COOK, WALTER W. *The Measurement of General Spelling Ability Involving Controlled Comparison between Techniques.* University of Iowa Studies in Education, Vol. 6, No. 6. The University, Iowa City.

'32 FISHER, R. A. *Statistical Methods for Research Workers*, Fourth Edition. Oliver and Boyd, Edinburgh.

'32 LENTZ, THEODORE F.; HIRSHSTEIN, BERTHA; AND FINCH, F. H. "Evaluation of Methods of Evaluating Test Items." *Journal of Educational Psychology*, 23: 344–50.

'32 TOOPS, HERBERT A. AND ROYER, ELMER B. *Predicting Soldiers' School Marks: A Problem in the Selection of Tests.* Ohio College Association Bulletin, No. 80. Ohio State University, Columbus.

'32 WOLFE, JACK. "The 'Consistency' of Intelligence Test Questions as a Supplement to Their Validity in Selecting the Best Items." Unpublished Master's Thesis. School of Education, College of the City of New York.

'33 OSBURN, W. J. "The Selection of Test Items." *Review of Educational Research*, 3: 21–32, 62–65.

'34 HORST, PAUL. "Increasing the Selection Efficiency of Personnel Tests." *Personnel Journal*, 12: 254–59.

'34 HORST, PAUL. "Item Analysis by the Method of Successive Residuals." *Journal of Experimental Education*, 2: 254–63.